Learn To Play The Drum Set
Drum Book with Accompanying Videos

ON THE DRUMS
Lesson Plan

MICHAEL FAETH

Watch accompanying videos at:

onthedrumslessons.com

Second Edition

ISBN: 979-8-9879431-9-9
Independently Published in Fresno, CA
onthedrumslessons.com

SESSION 1

Table of Contents

Dedication

The name of this book is dedicated to the great Fresno, CA musician, Nate Butler. He has a program entitled *The Local Show* on college radio station KFSR, and every time he names the members of a group and gets to the drummer, he emphatically says, "ON THE DRUMS!!"

Introduction

This book gives you an easy tool to help you get started playing the drum set. You can go through the book by yourself, but it is recommended to have a drum instructor for the benefit of getting their feedback and help along the way. The four categories I believe you need to cover to become a drummer are: drumming foundation, drum beats, sticking patterns and drummer inspiration.

The book begins with an outline of the lesson plan and the following pages go through each area in well laid-out detail. Each lesson is easy to understand and the accompanying videos help to demonstrate them. The exercises include a checkbox next to them to be marked off when learned so you can keep track of your progress.

Session 1 covers areas that will build a strong rhythmic foundation onto which more complex drumming can be built. The lesson plan is to be spread over the course of about three months. Ideally, you will take a 30 minute drum lesson once a week with your instructor, practice on your own for at least 30 minutes a day for five days per week, and take one day off to rest and reflect.

This book will help new drummers grow in confidence and welcome them into the fun, rewarding, and exciting world of drumming!!

"I stay as relaxed as I can while practicing... It is a conscious effort to be relaxed while playing and it starts in the practice room." – Steve Smith

Lesson Plan

Student Name: _____   Start Date: _____

Drumming Foundation

Drum Set Components   Reading & Writing Music   Notes & Rests
Stick Technique   Counting   Time Signature
Positioning & Posture   Tempo & Metronome
Drum Tuning   Staff, Bars, & Measures

Drum Beats

Hi-hat Counting   Drum Beat Variation #1   All Beats with Crash on 1
Snare on 2 & 4   Drum Beat Variation #2   All Beats on Ride
Bass Drum on 1 & 3   Drum Beat Variation #3   All Beats on "&" Only
Drum Beat   Drum Beat Variation #4   All Beats Combination

Sticking Patterns

Singles   Buzz Roll
Doubles   Sticking Combination
Paradiddles

Drummer Inspiration

Playing to Songs   Drumming Resources
Instructor Additions   Inspirational Drummers
Drum Products

○ Yes, I have completed all of the above.

Completion Date: _____

Turn to page 22

Drumming Foundation

You will find that some things are very easy to do on the drum set. Other things are very challenging and require lots of discipline and practice. This book teaches a rhythmic foundation that you can build upon and use to take your drumming to whatever level you wish to. The greatest aspect of playing drums is creating and sharing music with others and having fun doing it. Let's get started in the fun, rewarding, and exciting world of drumming!!

Drum Set Components *(Watch Accompanying Video)*

Drum sets come in all different sizes and configurations, but at their core, most of them consist of the components listed below. Check off the items you can identify and hit the drums and cymbals to hear how they sound:

○ Drumsticks	○ Crash cymbal	○ Cymbal stands	○ Snare wires
○ Snare drum	○ Ride cymbal	○ Drum heads	○ Snare strainer
○ Bass drum	○ Snare drum stand	○ Drum hoops	○ Drum throne
○ Hi-hat	○ Hi-hat stand	○ Drum key	
○ Rack tom	○ Hi-hat clutch	○ Tension rods	
○ Floor tom	○ Bass drum pedal	○ Lugs	

Stick Technique *(Watch Accompanying Video)*

There are different ways to hold the drum sticks. For our purposes, we will be using what is called "matched grip", where both hands hold the sticks in the same way.

Use your thumb, index finger, and middle finger to grip the stick in a relaxed manner, about 5 inches up from the bottom of the stick. The pinky and ring finger curl in lightly around the stick. Hold the sticks in front of you with your thumbs facing up and then rotate your wrists slightly so you can see some of the top of your hand. This is a good starting position for stick technique. When you strike the drums, the motion involves the sticks moving in your hand in a whipping fashion and comes primarily from wrist movement as opposed to holding the stick tightly and using only your arms.

None of this is to be adhered to rigidly, because as you move around the drum set, you may need to adjust your grip. The most important aspects to technique are playing relaxed, efficiently, and in a way that avoids injury. Also, sticks come in different sizes, so use ones that are comfortable for you. My favorite drumsticks are the Los Angeles 5A Wood model made by Vater.

○ Yes, I have an understanding of stick technique.

Positioning & Posture *(Watch Accompanying Video)*

Ultimately you will find out what works best for you with positioning and posture at the drum set, but here is a general guide to start from. The first step is to set your drum throne height. Try and sit where your thighs are pointed down at a very slight angle and keep your back straight. Next, position the bass drum and pedal in front of you and slightly to the right (if playing a right-handed set up; opposite if left-handed). Your shin should angle a small degree out towards the drum when your foot is on the pedal. Now do the same thing with hi-hat stand so your foot rests comfortably on the foot board. Try playing the bass drum and hi-hat with your heel up.

Next position the snare in between your legs with the top of it being about equal to belt level. You can tilt the snare drum towards you slightly. Move the rack tom around on the holder until it is in good striking distance and at the right angle. Place the floor tom to the right of the bass drum bringing it in close enough to comfortably reach.

Now bring in the crash cymbal and ride cymbal where you can reach them comfortably, including the bell of the ride. Once you have the entire drum set in place, make any final adjustments you may want to.

Right-handed players will usually play the hi-hat with their right hand while playing the snare drum with the left hand, crossing arms with the left going underneath. This would be opposite for left-handed players. But choose a way that makes sense to you.

When playing the drums, wear a comfortable pair of shoes that lace up and avoid flip flops or slide sandals.

○ **Yes, I have an understanding of positioning and posture.**

Drum Tuning *(Watch Accompanying Video)*

When it comes to tuning drums, it is entirely up to you in terms of the overall sound, but here is a general guide. When you first put on a new drum head, try your best to tighten each tension rod equally. You can use your fingers to start tightening them and then use a drum key. I find it easiest to use two drum keys at a time, gradually tightening opposite sides as you move in one direction around the drum. If you have a top head and a bottom head, try tuning the bottom to a medium tightness and the top head just a bit tighter. If you are tuning a drum head with an older drum head, loosen it up completely and then start to re-tighten it.

Some drummers like to use muffling on their drums, especially the bass drum. It is common to use a pillow or blanket stuffed inside a bass drum. Your snare and toms can be muffled by using tape or different muffling products. Ringo Starr famously added tea towels on top of his toms for some of the Beatles recordings, which created a very dry thud sound. Other drummers like Billy Cobham, Steve Smith, and Simon Phillips have very resonant toms with no muffling used.

The sound of drums can be changed drastically by using effects when recording, too. The iconic drum part heard during "In The Air Tonight" by Phil Collins was achieved by using a gated reverb effect.

○ **Yes, I have an understanding of how to tune drums.**

Writing & Reading Music

Just like a story can be told with using words, music can be shared with other musicians by writing it down using musical notation on sheet music. Let's explore some of the ways that is accomplished.

Counting

When you listen to music and naturally feel where you can clap, snap your fingers, or tap you foot, you can also count. If you exactly double the speed of your counting or cut it in half, the count will still follow right along with the music. One of the most common counts in music is 4 with it repeating like this:

1   2   3   4   1   2   3   4   1   2   3   4 ...

The duration it takes to count to 4 will be the length of a measure, which we will discuss soon. To double the counting speed, you add "and" in between like this:

1 + 2 + 3 + 4 + 1 + 2 + 3 + 4 + 1 + 2 + 3 + 4 + ...

A NOTE ABOUT COUNTING:
Counting can be very helpful when learning a drum part, but when it is time to play and perform, put it aside and just feel the music.

Tempo & Metronome

As you know, some songs are fast, some are slow. The speed of a song is called the tempo. The way we measure tempo is by **Beats Per Minute (BPM)**. You can use a metronome to set an audible click at different tempos.

Staff, Bars &, Measures

Just like a story uses sentences, paragraphs, and punctuation, music can be written and read using musical notation. Let's look at some of the tools used. Music notation is written on a staff consisting of 5 horizontal lines and the spaces:

Staff

Sheet music for drums usually includes a percussion clef like this, aka, drum clef or neutral clef.

The staff is divided into sections using vertical bars to make measures:

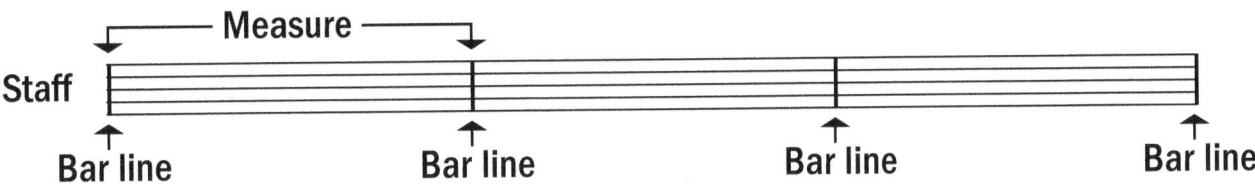

Notes & Rests

Just like words use letters to form different sounds, musical notation uses notes and rests to do this. Here are some to get familiar with for our purposes:

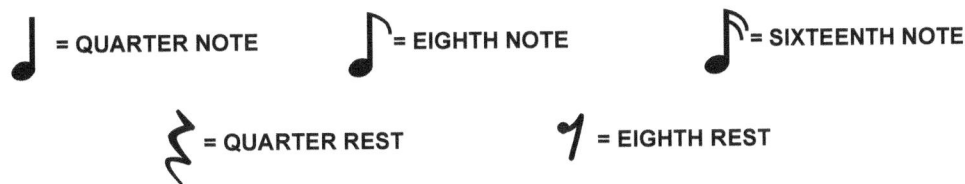

Each note and rest has a duration value in relation to a measure. Where the note is placed on the staff determines what sound is played. For instance:

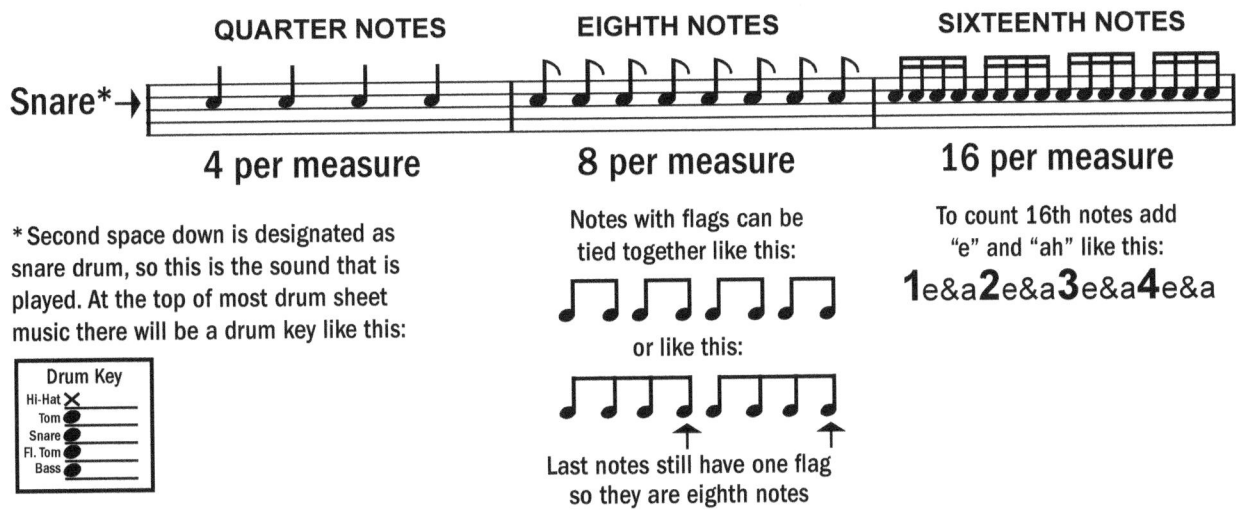

QUARTER NOTES	EIGHTH NOTES	SIXTEENTH NOTES
4 per measure	8 per measure	16 per measure

Snare*→

* Second space down is designated as snare drum, so this is the sound that is played. At the top of most drum sheet music there will be a drum key like this:

Drum Key
Hi-Hat ✕
Tom ●
Snare ●
Fl. Tom ●
Bass ●

Notes with flags can be tied together like this:

or like this:

Last notes still have one flag so they are eighth notes

To count 16th notes add "e" and "ah" like this:
1e&a**2**e&a**3**e&a**4**e&a

For rests, there is silence for whatever value is designated. For instance:

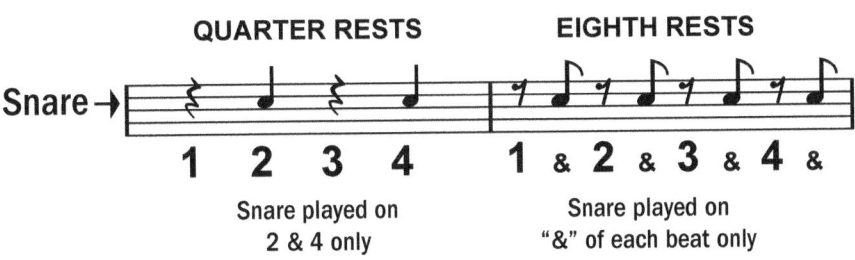

QUARTER RESTS	EIGHTH RESTS
1 2 3 4	**1** & **2** & **3** & **4** &
Snare played on 2 & 4 only	Snare played on "&" of each beat only

Time Signature

In order to know how many beats (counts) are in a measure and what kind of note makes up one count, we need to look at the time signature. Let's identify what it is and how to read it. A time signature will appear at the beginning of a piece of music and will be included in the staff like this:

The example above has a time signature of 4/4. This is how to read it:

4 = Top number tells you that there are 4 counts in every measure

4 = Bottom number tells you that it is a quarter note that is counted

So a measure might look like this:

Here is another example:

6 = Top number tells you that there are 6 counts in every measure

8 = Bottom number tells you that it is an eighth note that is counted

So a measure might look like this:

○ Yes, I have an understanding of reading and writing music.

Drum Set Playing

Okay, now it is time for the real fun to begin!! Let's apply some of what we have learned to the drum set. Go to the next page to get started.

"Repetition is the mother of skill." – Benny Grebb

Drum Beats *(Watch Accompanying Videos)*

Hi-hat Counting 65 ◯ 105 ◯

In drum notation different symbols can be used. Below an "x" is used for the hi-hat. The two dots in combination with the thin and thick double line at the end of the last measure is a repeat mark, so play a total of eight measures. Using a metronome, start at **65 BPM** and work your way incrementally up to **105 BPM**. Count eighth notes out loud for one free measure, i.e., **1 & 2 & 3 & 4 &**, and then start playing this music, ending on the "&" of four in the eighth measure:

Snare on 2 & 4 65 ◯ 105 ◯

Stems of notes can also point down. On counts two and four, the hands play in unison at the same time. Count one measure out loud and then play this music:

Bass Drum on 1 & 3 65 ◯ 105 ◯

Count one measure out loud and then play this music:

Drum Beat 65 ◯ 105 ◯

You are now ready to play your first drum beat!! It is to be inferred that the bass drum and snare drum notes are to be read together, so no rests are used. Count one measure out loud and then play this music:

Drum Beat Variation #1   65 ◯ 105 ◯

I refer to this beat as the "3 +" variation, because of the bass drum pattern. Count one measure out loud and then play this music:

Drum Beat Variation #2   65 ◯ 105 ◯

I refer to this beat as the "+ 3" variation, because of the bass drum pattern. Note that the snare and bass notes are tied together. Count one measure out loud and then play this music:

Drum Beat Variation #3   65 ◯ 105 ◯

I refer to this beat as the "+ " variation, because of the bass drum pattern. Note that this beat may feel strange because there is no bass drum on the one. Count one measure out loud and then play this music:

Drum Beat Variation #4   65 ◯ 105 ◯

I refer to this beat as the "all bass" variation, because of the bass drum pattern. Count one measure out loud and then play this music:

Drum Beat with Crash on 1   65 ◯   105 ◯

Same as before, but just add a crash cymbal. The symbol is different for the crash cymbal and it appears on a line above the normal staff.

Variation #1 with Crash on 1   65 ◯   105 ◯

Same as before, but just add a crash cymbal.

Variation #2 with Crash on 1   65 ◯   105 ◯

Same beat as before, but just add a crash cymbal.

Variation #3 with Crash on 1   65 ◯   105 ◯

Same beat as before, but just add a crash cymbal. This one will feel very strange because there will be a cymbal with no bass drum on the one. Cymbals are almost always played with a bass drum to give them more emphasis, but there are no rules in drumming other than to be musical. If a part calls for just a cymbal, then go for it.

Variation # 4 with Crash on 1   65 ⚪ 105 ⚪

Same beat as before, but just add a crash cymbal.

Drum Beat on Ride   65 ⚪ 105 ⚪

Same beat as before, but on ride cymbal, which is designated as top line of staff.

Variation #1 on Ride   65 ⚪ 105 ⚪

Same beat as before, but on ride cymbal.

Variation #2 on Ride   65 ⚪ 105 ⚪

Same beat as before, but on ride cymbal.

Variation #3 on Ride   65 ⚪ 105 ⚪

Same beat as before, but on ride cymbal.

Variation #4 on Ride 65 ○ 105 ○

Same beat as before, but on ride cymbal.

Drum Beat on "&" Only 65 ○ 105 ○

Same beat as before, but with hi-hat on "&"s only. This may be the most challenging section because there is a lot of independence required.

Variation #1 on "&" Only 65 ○ 105 ○

Same beat as before, but with hi-hat on "&"s only.

Variation #2 on "&" Only 65 ○ 105 ○

Same beat as before, but with hi-hat on "&"s only.

Variation #3 on "&" Only 65 ○ 105 ○

Same beat as before, but with hi-hat on "&"s only. No sounds are played on 1 or 3.

Variation #4 on "&" Only   65 ○   105 ○

Same beat as before, but with hi-hat on "&"s only.

All Beats Combination   65 ○   105 ○

Now we will combine the drum beat and the variations and play them all together. Each version will get four measures, so you will play a total of 20 measures. The thin and thick double line at the end of the last measure tells you it is the end of the composition and there is no repeat.

"Never be afraid to play simply." – Simon Phillips

Sticking Patterns *(Watch Accompanying Videos)*

There are two main areas drummers can practice, and those are the drum set and sticking patterns, or rudiments. Use a practice pad for sticking exercises to avoid being distracted with the desire to play the set. The goal is to get each hand to sound even. Good sticking technique translates to better facility on the drum set.

Singles 45 ○ 65 ○

With singles, each hand will play a single stroke alternating back and forth. Count 16th notes out loud for one free measure, i.e., **1**e&a**2**e&a**3**e&a**4**e&a, and then start playing . Start at **45 BPM** and work your way incrementally up to **65 BPM**. The "R" and "L" tells you which hand to use. For all of these sticking exercises, after doing the first four measures starting with your right hand, rest for one measure and then do four measures starting with your left hand.

RLRLRLRLRLRLRL...
LRLRLRLRLRLRLR...

Doubles 45 ○ 65 ○

With doubles, each hand plays two notes and alternates back and forth. Here is where you can really see how a relaxed grip helps the stick bounce off of the head and makes doing two notes in succession easier.

RRLLRRLLRRLLRRLL...
LLRRLLRRLLRRLLRR...

Paradiddles 45 ○ 65 ○

This rudiment is unique in that it combines singles and doubles together and alternates which hand starts the next beat.

RLRRLRLLRLRRLRLL...
LRLLRLRRLRLLRLRR...

Buzz Roll   45 ○   65 ○

The sound of a buzz roll is iconic. The grip used involves more pressure between the index finger and thumb to keep the sticks sort of pushed down, bouncing multiple times very close to the head.

It is helpful to realize that underneath a buzz roll is a series of single strokes, but since each stroke is a buzz it produces an almost continuous tone. The number of strokes depends on the tempo. For instance, for the two tempos we are using:

The duration we will play will be quarter note rolls, so we end up with two buzz rolls per measure. I find it useful to count this like **oneeeeeee, two... threeeeeee, four.** The notation for the buzz roll uses a "Z" on the stem of a note and a tie to a second note. The hand you start the roll on will be the hand that ends it. The first stroke will be a buzz and the last one will be a single stroke.

Sticking Combination   45 ○   65 ○

Now we will combine the sticking patterns and play them all together. Each version will get four measures, so you will play a total of 16 measures for each hand. Start with your right hand first, rest for one measure, and then start with your left.

Playing To Songs

One of the best ways to get better on the drum set is to play along to some of your favorite songs. From what you have learned so far, select some songs that you think you might be able to play. The goal is to play the song from beginning to the end, even if all of the parts are not played exactly like the record. Just keep a solid beat all the way through. Write down what you like about the music and the drum part and make any notes related to learning it.

Song Title _____ Artist: _____

Notes:

Song Title _____ Artist: _____

Notes:

Song Title _____ Artist: _____

Notes:

○ Yes, I have played drums along to the songs above.

Instructor Additions

Below is an area for additional exercises to be added.

Exercise #1 _____

Exercise #2 _____

Exercise #3 _____

○ Yes, I have completed these additional exercises.

Drum Products

There are many companies making great drum products. Below are some I am familiar with and would recommend.

Rogers drums	Remo heads & drums	Paiste cymbals
Ludwig drums	Tama hardware	Istanbul cymbals
Gretsch drums	Vater drumsticks	Sabian cymbals
DW bass drum pedal	Zildjian cymbals	Evans practice pads

Drummer Resources

Below are some resources definitely worth checking out.

Gaddiments – *drum book of advanced sticking combinations by the legendary Steve Gadd*

Drumchannel.com – *online drum lessons, interviews, and performances by world class artists*

Drumeo.com – *drum lesson videos you can watch anytime with legendary drummers*

Hudsonmusic.com – *an abundance of digital and printed drumming material*

Onlinedrummer.com – *a vast collection of quality sheet music for drumming*

Soundbrenner – *a metronome app*

Inspirational Drummers

A small list of some drummers definitely worth checking out for inspiration:

Terry Bozzio	Gavin Harrison	Keith Carlock
Stewart Copeland	John Bonham	Rob Ellis
Neil Peart	Vinnie Colaiuta	Matt Chamberlain
Manu Katché	Sheila E.	Mike Peterson
Alan Myers	Steve Smith	Billy Cobham
Steve Gadd	Chad Wackerman	Gina Schock
Bill Bruford	Benny Grebb	JD Beck
Tony Williams	Anika Nilles	Devon Taylor
Buddy Rich	Antonio Sanchez	Cindy Blackman
Louie Bellson	Chris Coleman	Hannah Ford-Welton
Mark Guiliana	Jack DeJohnette	Milos Branisavljevic

○ Yes, I have checked out some of these products, resources, and drummers.

Thank you!!

To all of the amazing musicians and drummers that have inspired me along my journey playing the drum set. To the friends and family that took the photos that appear on the next page. To Joe Lizama and John Koontz for providing me with valuable feedback on the first edition.

Interested in helping make this book better? Submit your suggestions and comments at:

onthedrumslessons.com

Circa 1982 – I started out playing drums in my mom's bedroom closet. We lived in a mobile home with thin walls and I can't recall her complaining about the noise. I am grateful she gave me the freedom to practice!! Pictured is the 2nd drum set I had, a gift from a family friend. The first set was also a gift and used three snare drums without snares as makeshift toms. You play what you have.

Circa 1987 – I played on a completely electronic drum set with only a Roland Octopad and bass drum triggering sounds from a drum machine.

Circa 1996 – Here I am playing a classic 4-piece set, which included 1960's Ludwig Club Date gold sparkle toms and bass drum along with a 1960's Rogers Tower Model snare drum.

Circa 2000 – Set up at Wolfsound Audio in Fresno, CA to record drum tracks with the largest drum set I ever compiled. The set included electronic pads, stacked cymbals, Nyabinghi and Dundun drums, tambourine, mini hi-hats, Ribbon Crasher, Vibratone, African bells, and an 18" Rototom.

2014 – Here I am playing a very stripped down kit with just bass drum, snare, hi-hat, and cymbals.

2022 – My drum kit used for recording in our Love Shack Studios in Fresno, CA.

Notes

Take notes on anything related to your drumming:

_____

_____

_____

_____

_____

_____

_____

_____

_____

_____

_____

_____

_____

_____

_____

_____

_____

_____

_____

_____

"The drums have a lot to say. You know, I've always felt that the drums are as passionate, and can be played as tenderly, as any instrument, as romantic as say a violin. It just takes the right setting to do it and to be able to express those feelings." – Tony Williams

Certificate of Completion

Congratulations!!

You have completed the lesson plan for *Session 1*. Continue striving to be the best drummer you can be.

Are you able to play relaxed and efficiently? Do you play with a nice groove and have a good "feel"? Even the most experienced drummer needs to keep those things in mind.

Keep having fun with your practicing and playing. May you always stay inspired and create some amazing music "ON THE DRUMS!"

Be well,

Michael

PS: If you found this book helpful, please share it.

Cut along dotted line to remove and frame the 5" x 7" Certificate of Completion